The Way to Steal Freedom

The Guide for Government

Ron Paul Jones

To steal freedom, do whatever this book says.

Purge government officials and opposition leaders

Purge government officials who do not agree with government policy. These officials are more likely to sabotage their work and undermine the government. Keep detailed personnel files on these officials, including personal information like background, associate connections, and work history. Identify negative portions of their personnel files that will be most damaging to their reputation and credibility. Use the press and media to create distorted pictures of them. Alienate these troublemakers from their supporters. Pressure them to resign their positions.

Treat opposition leaders and groups similarly. Keep detailed personnel files that can be used to damage their reputation and credibility. Use the press and media to create unfavorable perceptions of them or their group. Find technicalities where they violated the rules or laws. Apprehend them or remove their ability to function, if necessary, by arresting them or revoking their licenses. Do not merely alienate these troublemakers from their supporters. Alienate them from the general population and possible sympathizers as well. Some of these opposition leaders and groups have no real position to resign, so their reputation is everything. Destroy their reputation and demonize them in order to remove their ability to cause more trouble.

Attack laws and constitution

Laws and constitution provide a guide of what the government can do, not what it cannot do. Likewise, laws and constitution limit what the people can do. Aggressively attack both when the words, meanings, and intentions are unclear. Use government lawyers to parse the words to provide as much room for the government to limit the freedom of the people. Enforce the laws and constitution to the limit. Always assume that laws and constitution allow the government to do anything unless it explicitly states otherwise.

Take advantage of opportunities

Be aware of the latest events and news occurring throughout the country and world. Take advantage of political opportunities to gain support. When there is a disaster or crisis, magnify the crisis when the government is able to keep the situation under control. Downplay the crisis when the situation gets out of hand. Blame others, like scapegoats or enemies, when necessary. Use the media as a helpful tool to feed this information to the people.

Blame scapegoats,
foreign and domestic

Scapegoats provide a useful way to divert attention away from the country's failures and weaknesses. Foreign scapegoats include other countries that are doing better. If the economy fails, blame another country for not playing fair. It is usually better to blame a country with a different culture. After all, people have a natural tendency to distrust or dislike things that are different and people who are different. Play the race card, ethnic card, or any other xenophobic card. But do so subtly because playing too hard will make the population suspicious. People might catch on to the scapegoat tactics, making future use of scapegoats less credible and less effective.

Domestic scapegoats can also divert attention away from the country's failures and weakness. If the economy is weak and the unemployment is high, blame illegal immigrants for stealing jobs. It is easy to blame illegal immigrants because they entered the country by breaking the law. The illegal immigrants also work while in the country, so there is a perception that they steal jobs. Many times, illegal immigrants work for lower wages as well, which pushes everyone's wages lower, and this is upsetting for many regular working people. Like with foreign scapegoats, use whatever xenophobic card is necessary, but do not play too hard.

Remember, the goal of using scapegoats is to divert attention away from the country's failures and weaknesses by placing blame on others. Ideally, the blame is directed towards those who are different. When the people blame scapegoats more, they will blame the government less.

Use the military in domestic crises

Use the military in domestic crises whenever possible. Domestic crises could include environmental disasters like earthquakes, hurricanes, floods, and droughts. They could also include domestic disturbances like riots and revolts. Use the military to assist with natural disasters to make the people more willing to accept the use of military forces to control or put down domestic disturbances. When using the military in any of these situations, make it clear that the military has top command over operations. Progress slowly when using the military in domestic crises. Do not overwhelm the people with a huge military presence initially because it will frighten them. Start first by providing logistical support with the environmental disasters. Later use the actual military when local agencies are incompetent and the public demands military intervention. Use this same approach for domestic disturbances. Start providing logistical support. Later use the full military to suppress riots or revolts. Issue emergency alerts and curfew orders to scare the population. Do not hesitate to take away the people's rights when necessary. For example, leave the following options open: suspend free speech and habeas corpus, control the press with censorship, and declare martial law.

Create domestic wars everywhere

One of the best ways to strengthen the government's authority is by creating domestic wars everywhere. Creating wars give people the perception that it is the government's responsibility to fight these wars. The enemy in these wars can be almost anyone or anything. For example, the government could wage wars against Drugs, Terror, Obesity, Crime, and Piracy. The main benefit for creating these types of wars is that the wars are ongoing and have no real end in sight. The enemies can never be totally beat because these types of enemies are ideas that cannot totally surrender. Be sure to play to the people's senses. For example, for the war on drugs, terror, and crime, exploit the people's fear and need for security. For the war on obesity, make the goal of healthier children the focus of the war. For the war on piracy, play the security card by tying terrorists and gangs to piracy.

People will become accustomed to the idea of the government fighting these wars. They will demand updates and figures relating to the wars. The people will turn to the government for results, at the expense of the local government and local law enforcement. The perception that the government is responsible for fighting these wars will make it easier to add the costs of the wars to the national budget. Because these are domestic wars, the people will be more willing to see increases in tax revenues devoted to fighting the wars.

Keep the people under
close surveillance

Start an aggressive surveillance program. Keeping a close eye on the people will cause them to live in fear. It will cast a dark shadow over people's lives. Close surveillance will make the people afraid and indecisive to take actions that might go against the will of the government. People will be afraid to speak their minds in public, to assemble in groups, to protest against things they feel are not right. Close surveillance will keep the majority of the people in line, and it will break the spirit of aspiring leaders of the people. Surveillance can take many forms. Some of the better ones include:

National ID Card: A national ID card will help keep track of people. It can be used as a standard form of ID used to travel overseas. Then the program can be expanded to domestic travel, first to planes and trains that travel from city to city. People are already used to providing ID on planes and trains, so they should be more agreeable to providing a national ID card to travel on planes and trains. Later expand the national ID to travel on the roads. Use the national ID as a valid form of driver's license or ID for checkpoints. If the local governments do not accept the national ID, pressure them by launching an advertising campaign to take the issue directly to the people. Play the national security and illegal immigrant card. Tell the people that the national ID card will help the government find enemies of the nation, as well as identify those who are not citizens or legal residents. But be careful with using these trump cards. If the cards are used too often or if the messages are too over-the-top, people might get suspicious of the government's intentions. If this fails to convince the people, stress the convenience of a national ID card. After all, people tend to value their time. Be sure to highlight the hassles people will have to go through if they do not have a national ID card. After a few years, the national ID can be used for public dealings with the government like filing taxes, as well as with private transactions like shopping a the store. Eventually when the technology permits, a tracking device can be integrated into the national ID card to track people's movements and purchases.

RPM (Reading people's minds): Reading people's minds does not require the use of psychics or fortune-tellers. It requires a collaboration of the government with businesses. Try to "persuade" businesses to get them to provide information. It is in the government's best interest to find out everything about the people, including their reading and viewing habits. Pressure businesses to provide information about what their customers are reading. Find out what people are buying from the bookstore. Find out what people are reading on the internet. The internet will provide a powerful and efficient tool to track people's reading habits. Reading the people's minds through the radio and television is not as efficient yet. But technology will soon catch up with the growth of digital radio and digital cable television. This will make it easier to find out what a person has watched in the past or want to watch in the future. If the growth of digital radio or television is not moving along fast enough, consider passing laws that promote digital radio and television. Create a digital standard for the media and also for the media hardware manufacturers.

Surveillance of communication: Unless they are hermits or enjoy living in isolated bubbles, people communicate with each other. They talk to family, friends, co-workers, or anyone willing to listen. Listen in to the people's telephone conversations. Monitor their email and text messages. Gather phone histories to find out who they are talking to on the phone. Track their cell phone GPS movements to find out who they are meeting. Monitor internet chat rooms and message boards. Monitor social networking sites to find out who their friends are.

VIP surveillance: Keep in mind that most of the people are harmless to the government. Monitor the important people more closely. These include government officials, opposition leaders, celebrities, business leaders, civic leaders, and church leaders. Anyone who is a leader is a potential threat to the power of the government. Leaders have the ability to mobilize people quickly. Without the leaders, the people will have less motivation and less direction to cause trouble.

Embrace tracking technologies

Embrace technologies that help keep track of people. People fall in two groups: they are either troublemakers or potential troublemakers. Keep track of the people's movements. Install cameras at traffic lights and capture the license plate information. Tell the people that these cameras help make the roads safer by deterring bad driving behavior. Maintain a database of biometric information, including fingerprints. Try to entice people to voluntarily give their fingerprints to the government. Require that professional licenses and identification cards include fingerprint data. Promote the use of biometrics for consumer transactions by telling the people that biometrics make transactions safer and faster. Create a system to track cellphone and other wireless devices. People voluntarily carry cell phones and wireless devices, so gathering information on people carrying these devices will be less intrusive.

On the offline world, monitor the internet. Create fake people and identifications and communicate with the people. Create traps and bait the people into becoming troublemakers or criminals. Maintain records of all communications in case the records are needed in court. Do not assume anyone is "puffing" on the internet; take every word seriously. Be sure to inject fake people into all types of websites, like forums, message boards, chat rooms, and social networking sites.

Any technology that helps the government keep track of the people is a good technology.

Pass hate crime laws

Pass hate crime laws to achieve the government's public relations goals. People will have the perception that the government is strongly against discrimination. This will make the people blind to the government's intention of diminishing the importance of individuals. Hate crime laws make groups of people more important, at the expense of individuals. For the government to steal freedom, it needs to steal freedom from individuals. The population must have pride in being a group of people, instead of having pride of being unique individuals. Any time the population think of themselves as a group of people instead of as individuals, it is good for the government. It softens the people up for policies and laws that promote the good of the people, the good of society, and the good of the country. They will then believe that it is the people's role to serve the government, instead of the government's role to serve the people.

Maintain terrorist lists, immigrant lists, sexual offender lists, etc.

Because the population is so large, it is very difficult to maintain a central database of all people. Start by tracking potential terrorists, illegal immigrants, and sexual offenders. The public will support the government's plans to set up a central database consisting of all types of personal information and biometrics on these groups of people. Take advantage of this opportunity to build the database, test it, and improve it. Get fingerprint data from law enforcement agencies. For people who do not have criminal records or fingerprint files, find creative ways to gather the missing information. For example, require all airline passengers to provide their fingerprints as a matter of national security. Make fingerprinting part of standard background checks. When technology permits, expand the database to include biometric data, like eye positions, body scans, palm scans, voice scans, and DNA codes. Slowly expand the database to include all criminals. The eventual goal is for the database to include all people. It is important to proceed slowly, so the people will not realize what it happening until it is too late for them to stop it.

Take away people's property

Make the people less secure by taking away their property. One way to take away their property is through taxes, which is discussed in another section. This section focuses on taking the people's property for government purposes, or eminent domain. This is one area that requires the local government's help. Give the local government tax revenues earmarked for local improvements. The local government will use some the revenues to take away the people's property. It is best to not take away the property outright, but to compensate the owners for the seizure. This way, the government will not have to deal with landowner protests or uprisings. Wage an effective public relations campaign to highlight the benefits of the seizure. Two benefits that are known to be successful are an increase in jobs and an improved infrastructure. Allow private corporations to align with the government to seize property to create private enterprises that will create jobs for the people.

When the people have less property, they will have less stake in the country. They will have less to lose, so they will be weaker in their opposition to government policies. Remember that property and power are strongly related. People with no property or property rights will feel less powerful. They will become more dependent on the government, which will make them easier to control.

Control education

Keeping total control over the people for many years can be a difficult task. To make it easier for the government to accomplish this, it is necessary for the government to control education. The government should directly decide the curriculum for pre-school through university schools. Teach the children according to what is in the best interest of the government. This way, the government will be able to manage education to turn out the type of students needed by the country at any given time. For example, expand physical education and junior military programs to make students more prepared to join the military. Or stress certain sciences to improve military technology. Controlling education also allows the government to brainwash the children so that they will have very strong nationalist feelings and strong desires to follow the rules and laws. When these children grow up, they will love the country so much that they will be blind to the government's control over them. Nationalistic, law-abiding people are less likely to be troublemakers and will be much easier to control.

Expand military draft

The government cannot have total control with an all-volunteer military. An all-volunteer military is dangerous because it is based on freedom. In an all-volunteer military, the people have the freedom to determine how they want to live and whether they want to join the military and put their lives at risk. The all-volunteer military must be replaced with a military that includes some level of required service. Create a military draft program to be put in place in case the nation is fighting a war. Allow the military draft to be implemented for foreign wars, not just defensive wars. Ensure that the military draft program includes all young adults, men and women. Take away the people's freedom early on by forcing them to join the military or other similar organization directly controlled by the government. Set the duration of service for a certain amount of time, at least two years. It is important that the people understand early on that the government owns them. They must realize that the government can have control over their lives any time it wants to. That is why the military draft is necessary.

Engage in aggressive interrogation and torture

Like the suspension of habeas corpus, the threat of aggressive interrogation and torture will reduce the numbers of people in opposition of the government. When interrogating people, threaten them and their families in order to gather other names of suspected enemies of the government. This will set up a chain reaction where the government will have a regular flow of enemies to interrogate and arrest. When it is apparent that some people will not crack under the pressure of the interrogation, use more extreme methods. Consider torture as a tool to gain valuable information. Fear is a powerful weapon to control the people. Word about the interrogation and torture methods will spread quickly. The majority of the people will be very afraid to oppose the government. Even the die-hard opposition members will hesitate to cause trouble.

Suspend habeas corpus

A very effective way to silence the opposition is to suspend habeas corpus. Start by arresting true enemies of the state, including traitors and terrorists. Keep them in prison without charges or a court trial. Gradually, suspend habeas corpus to domestic enemies of the government, including citizens and residents. Label the citizens and residents as traitors and terrorists. Treat them as enemies of the state by also keeping them in prison without charges or court trial. Fight the civilian court system, and if necessary put these enemies of the government before a military court. Do not hesitate to round up any people suspected of being enemies, and be willing to round up completely innocent people. This reminder of the possibility of imprisonment will keep the people in a constant state of fear.

Limit free speech and assembly

Free speech provides the catalyst for the people to protest against the government. Free speech will lead to assembly of the people to join mass protests. Limit both free speech and assembly, and it will be much easier to control the people. Assemble a domestic spy network of government workers to keep watch over the people. Inject government spies into the towns and cities to pose as ordinary residents. Be sure to infiltrate key businesses and local governments. Keep ordinary people in line by enlisting citizens into the spy network to spy on their family and friends. Be sure that the people know they are being spied on. Use the media to report the arrest of enemies of the government. Execute random search warrants on the people's homes. When the people are fully aware of the spy network, they will become more paranoid and afraid. They will be less willing to speak out or act against the government. There will be fewer troublemakers for the government to worry about.

Control media through censorship

Controlling the media is essential to maintaining total control over the people. Censorship of the media is essential because it is important for people to see only government-approved content. This will help to limit the people's views, and it helps to align the people's views with the government's views. Use propaganda to twist stories, distort truths, and spread lies. Bully the media executives and journalists to scare them into reporting unfavorable stories about the government. Keep a close watch over newspapers, radio stations, and television networks. Be especially attentive to the internet. Because the internet is difficult to monitor, considers shutting down whole websites so the people cannot view them. In emergency situations, shut down and completely black out the internet with an internet kill switch. Do this temporarily or else the people will have nothing else to do but cause trouble in the streets. Be sure to fill the void caused by any blackout with pro-government content.

Be careful of too much censorship or shutdown of media and internet, or both will lose credibility. The people must have some belief that the information is not biased. If the opposition is able to provide information that is damaging to the government and believable to the people, do not try to restrict or stop the information too strongly. This will give the opposition more standing and more credibility in the eyes of the people. Instead, spread misinformation by flooding the media and internet to counter the opposition. The goal is to confuse the people.

Require gun registration

Take the gun registration issue to the silent majority. The majority does not own guns, so these people should be the target audience to convince people that gun registration is a good thing. Promote how gun registration will help the government monitor guns better and keep guns out of the hands of criminals. Promise that gun registration will reduce crime and violence. Bring crime victims and law enforcement before the news media to help with promoting gun registration. Explain that the world will be a better place if only the government and law enforcement could keep guns. Be sure that the people realize that gun registration is a "common-sense" restriction. Do not attempt to require gun registration until the political climate is right, or the people will reject it. Eventually require that everyone register their guns.

Gun owners are the last defense against total government control. That is why it is a huge priority for the government to know who owns guns and where the guns are. Registration will allow the government to effectively track and monitor gun ownership. Even if many gun owners are not troublemakers in the eyes of the government, it is always possible for protests, insurrections, and revolts to occur. Under the right circumstances, a strong core of gun owners who value freedom too much, and with effective leaders could possibly mobilize a group of people to fight against the government. Gun registration will make it easier to identify these people and quickly arrest them when necessary.

Control guns through economic means

Remember the eventual goal is to restrict guns altogether. But steps must be taken slowly and lightly. First, use the government's economic power, such as the power to create inflation, to make guns and ammunition purchases unaffordable to many people. What good is the freedom to own guns when the people do not have the money to buy them? When people have to choose between the rising costs of food, housing, energy, and other necessities, they might be more willing to pass up on purchasing guns. In addition, those currently owning guns might be more willing give up their guns. Exploit this situation by orchestrating events to purchase guns directly from the population. Promote these events as events intended to keep the country safer.

Manage the economy

The successful government needs a stable economy. The economy can be a huge threat to the government's ability to maintain control. For example, a poor economy and high unemployment could cause unrest. Do not be afraid to use the government's power of the purse to manage the economy. Use the government's money to purchase goods and services that can support businesses and create jobs. Government money can also be used to purchase and maintain stockpiles of food, oil, and other commodities to control prices when prices become too volatile.

Be ready to intervene in the marketplace. It is in the best interest of the government to have the support of big businesses. If a large business is about to fail, consider rescuing the business. Publicize the bailout as one that is necessary to maintain stability for the economy as a whole. Identify which big businesses are too big to fail. Be careful to support the big businesses that are political allies or potential allies. Realize that public opinion for some big businesses are unfavorable, so allow some of those businesses to fail. Assisting big businesses will come at the expense of small businesses. But because big businesses hold so much more economic power and clout, they make better political partners than small businesses. But try also to maintain good relations with small businesses because of their strength in numbers. Reach out to small business groups and be sure to earmark a significant portion of government purchases for small businesses.

Increase the income tax and inflation tax

Income is one factor of wealth. People with high incomes often are wealthier than those with low incomes. More wealth gives people peace of mind and the feeling of security. Take away their income or wealth and people will feel less free and less secure.

One effective way to take away the people's income is by levying a tax on income. By increasing the income tax, people will have to work more to feel more free and secure. Increasing the income tax will result in smaller savings for people and less wealth. Many people will feel the need to work just to keep up with daily expenses of living. Some will have to take on additional work. With more time devoted to worry and work, people will have less time to constructively challenge the government. They still might complain, but complaining does not cause too much harm for the government. Make people work more and they will cause less trouble. Be careful to not increase the income tax too much, or people will start not wanting to work. Too many people out of work will not only hurt the economy, it will also give people too much free time to cause trouble.

One way to take away the people's wealth is by inflation of money. Print more money to reduce the value of the money to create inflation. Allow the central bank to print more money, and allow the government to spend money it doesn't have. Pay off government expenses and obligations by printing even more money. This cycle of printing and spending money will lead to more inflation. The inflation reduces the country's money, making it more costly to purchase goods and services. This higher cost is passed on to the people like a tax: the inflation tax. The inflation tax is mostly hidden to people because they do not actually pay out of pocket for it. This stealth characteristic makes the inflation tax better to levy because many people either will not realize that the tax exists, or they will realize the tax exists but feel powerless to do anything about it. Like increasing the income tax, increasing the inflation tax will force people to work more to have more savings and wealth. Their free time is used for worrying more or working more. With less free time, the people will have less time to cause trouble.

Remember, the goal is to steal the people's freedom. Do any and all things necessary to accomplish this goal.